S N A P S H O T S I N H I S T O R Y

WATERGATE

Scandal in the White House

by Dale Anderson

WATERGATE

Scandal in the White House

by Dale Anderson

Content Adviser: Derek Shouba, Adjunct History Professor
and Assistant Provost, Roosevelt University

Reading Adviser: Katie Van Sluys, Ph.D.,
School of Education, DePaul University

COMPASS POINT BOOKS
MINNEAPOLIS, MINNESOTA

973.924
AND
TS4643

 ### Compass Point Books

3109 West 50th Street, #115
Minneapolis, MN 55410

Visit Compass Point Books on the Internet at
www.compasspointbooks.com
or e-mail your request to
custserv@compasspointbooks.com

For Compass Point Books
Jennifer VanVoorst, Jaime Martens, XNR Productions, Inc.,
Catherine Neitge, Keith Griffin, and Carol Jones

Produced by White-Thomson Publishing Ltd.

For White-Thomson Publishing
Stephen White-Thomson, Susan Crean, Amy Sparks,
Tinstar Design Ltd., Derek Shouba, Peggy Bresnick Kendler,
Laurel Haines, and Timothy Griffin

Library of Congress Cataloging-in-Publication Data
Anderson, Dale, 1953–
  Watergate : scandal in the White House / by Dale Anderson.
    p. cm. — (Snapshots in history)
  Includes bibliographical references and index.

  ISBN-13: 978-0-7565-2010-6 (hardcover)
  ISBN-10: 0-7565-2010-X (hardcover)

1. Watergate Affair, 1972–1974—Juvenile literature. 2. Nixon,
Richard M. (Richard Milhous), 1913–1994—Juvenile literature. 3.
United States—Politics and government—1969–1974—Juvenile
literature. I. Title. II. Series.
  E860.A64 2007
  973.924—dc22   2006004416

CONTENTS

Break-in and Arrests

Chapter

1

On the night of June 16, 1972, seven men gathered in Room 214 of the Watergate Hotel in Washington, D.C. On the sixth floor of one of the Watergate's six buildings was the headquarters of the Democratic National Committee (DNC). The seven men planned to break into these offices.

These men were not common thieves. One of the leaders, G. Gordon Liddy, was a former agent of the Federal Bureau of Investigation (FBI). The other leader, E. Howard Hunt, was retired from the Central Intelligence Agency (CIA). Their accomplices included James McCord, who carried bugs for telephones. Bernard Barker brought cameras to take pictures of DNC documents. Virgilio Gonzalez had tools to pick locks. Eugenio Martinez and Frank Sturgis served as guards.

The Watergate complex included a hotel in addition to apartment buildings and two office buildings.

9

The burglars had been hired by officials working for President Richard M. Nixon, a Republican. They hoped the phone bugs and photos would provide information that could be used to ensure Nixon's victory in the 1972 presidential election.

Before they entered the building, McCord placed tape across the latches on stairway doors on several floors. This would prevent the doors from locking, allowing the burglars to escape quickly if needed. That would prove a costly mistake.

THE CUBAN CONNECTION

Three of the burglars—Barker, Gonzalez, and Martinez—were Cuban-Americans who opposed Cuban leader Fidel Castro. Barker and Martinez had taken part in the failed Bay of Pigs invasion of Cuba in 1962. This attack, sponsored by the CIA, was an attempt to land a small force of anti-Castro Cubans on the island to launch a rebellion that would oust Castro. In preparing for the attack, they had met Hunt, a CIA planner at the time.

Liddy and Hunt stayed at the hotel while the other five made their move. The burglars had a walkie-talkie, or portable two-way radio, as did Liddy and Hunt. An eighth man—Alfred Baldwin—also had one. Stationed in a motel room across the street, he was a lookout, ready to radio in an alarm if he saw any sign of danger to the burglars.

As the burglars moved up a stairway toward the DNC offices, Frank Wills, a security guard for the office building, found one of the doorways McCord had taped. Wills removed the tape and called his supervisor, who told him to inspect the doors on other floors. Strangely, Wills stopped to eat instead.

G. Gordon Liddy had worked for the White House before becoming involved in the Watergate burglary.

While Wills ate, the burglars reached the sixth floor. They had trouble picking the lock on the door leading into the DNC offices, though. Eventually they had to take it off at its hinges. By this time, Wills had gone back to the garage level and had seen that the door was once again taped. One of the burglars had foolishly retaped it. Wills called the police.

11

The police car that arrived at the scene was unmarked, and the officers wore civilian clothes. For those reasons, Baldwin did not realize the men were police officers and did not alert the burglars. The officers met Wills in the basement and then took a stairway—a different one than that used by the burglars—up to the eighth floor. The officers went there first because of recent reports of attempted burglaries there.

By this time, the burglars were finally entering the DNC offices. Hearing some noise on another stairway, they shut off their walkie-talkie to prevent its static from alerting anyone to their presence. It was another mistake.

Meanwhile, the police had moved down to the sixth floor. Two had gone onto a terrace outside the DNC offices, where Baldwin could see them from across the street. Worried, he called Liddy and told him that unknown people with guns drawn were on the balcony.

Liddy tried to radio the burglars but could not get through. Minutes later—at 2:30 A.M. on June 17—the

Not the First Time

The June 17 break-in was not the first time the burglars had been to the DNC offices. Their first two attempts to break in—on Friday, May 26, and Saturday, May 27—both failed. On May 26, the burglars thought they saw an alarm that would go off. On May 27, their lock-picking tools did not work. However, the following day, on their third try, they were able to pick the lock and enter. They photographed some documents and planted bugs on two phones. The June 17 break-in was staged to replace one of those bugs, which did not work properly.

police entered the DNC offices and arrested the five burglars. Searching the suspects, the police found the wire-tapping equipment, two cameras, 40 rolls of film, and a few thousand dollars in cash. The cash was in $100 bills with consecutive serial numbers. That fact suggested that the burglars had been paid by someone who had taken the cash out of a bank and raised the possibility that the money could be traced through bank records. The police also found keys to two rooms in the Watergate Hotel. One was the room Liddy and Hunt were in—and were quickly abandoning. In their panic to leave, however, they left behind evidence to tie them to the burglary.

The five burglars were taken to the police station. They tried to hide their identities by giving the officers false names. Barker, for instance, said his name was Frank Carter, and McCord called himself Edward Martin. The police secured search warrants so they could check the rooms for evidence. They also called in the FBI because of the phone-tapping equipment, since illegal bugging is a federal crime.

While the police were processing the burglars, Hunt and Liddy got to work. Hunt visited a lawyer and, handing him $8,500 in cash, asked him to go to the police station and get the men out on bail. But the money Hunt gave the lawyer was not enough because the judge set bail at $30,000 or more for each person. As a result, the five burglars stayed in jail.

Liddy, meanwhile, had gone to his office. There, he spent hours shredding papers related to the burglary. Liddy was worried because he worked for the Committee to Re-elect the President (CREEP). CREEP was the official campaign committee set up to help Nixon, who was then the president of the United States, win reelection in 1972. Also, Liddy and Hunt had both worked at the White House itself. If word got out that White House and CREEP employees were involved in the burglary, the president would suffer.

But word would soon get out. After taking the fingerprints of the five burglars, the police discovered their true identities. This revealed the real name of McCord, who, it turned out, was the chief security officer at CREEP. On Monday, June 19, the news hit the papers. *The Washington Post* reported:

> *One of the five men arrested early Saturday in the attempt to bug the Democratic National Committee headquarters is the salaried security coordinator for President Nixon's re-election committee.*

Worse news for the Nixon administration was to follow. In the abandoned hotel rooms, police found address books that belonged to the burglars. Two listed Howard Hunt's name or initials, and two included notes near his name that said WH, referring to the White House. CREEP and the White House were quick to distance themselves from the burglary. Ron Zeigler, Nixon's press secretary, dismissed the incident as a third-rate burglary attempt. John Mitchell, the head of CREEP, denied any connection to the break-in.

Those denials were false. The burglars had been hired by officials working for Nixon who knew that news of this connection could damage the president politically. Behind the scenes, these officials began planning an elaborate and criminal cover-up to try to hide the truth. Within days, the president himself learned about and took part in this cover-up. Unraveling the deception would take the next two years. When that work finally ended, the third-rate burglary produced a stunning outcome— Richard M. Nixon's resignation as president of the United States. ◣

The information associated with "HH" in one of the burglar's address books matched the information for Howard Hunt in another, linking the burglary to Hunt — and to the White House.

15

Nixon and Politics

By 1972, Richard M. Nixon had spent more than two decades in national politics. In his first campaign in 1946, he ran as a Republican from California for a seat in the U.S. House of Representatives. He immediately showed he was a tough and, some would say, unfair campaigner. He won by linking his Democratic opponent with communists, a political curse at the time.

In the House of Representatives, Nixon gained fame for his intense questioning of Alger Hiss, a former member of the State Department whom Nixon charged with being a spy for the Soviet Union. In 1950, Nixon won a seat in the U.S. Senate, once again attacking his opponent as being a communist.

In a televised speech in 1952, Richard Nixon denied taking illegal gifts. He did admit, though, that he had accepted the gift of a pet dog named Checkers for his two daughters.

In 1952, Republicans selected World War II hero Dwight D. Eisenhower as their candidate for president. Eisenhower picked Nixon as his running mate to add youth to the ticket. But Nixon's rise to vice president was threatened by stories that he had spent some campaign money on personal uses. Nixon defended himself in a national television address, and Eisenhower kept him. The team won in 1952 and again in 1956.

Nixon ran for president against John F. Kennedy in 1960. He narrowly lost the election. Despite the possibility of voter fraud in Illinois and Texas, which were both Kennedy wins, Nixon accepted the outcome. He went home to California, defeated and bitter.

Two years later, he tried to become governor of California. Again, Nixon lost the race. Many experts felt that he would retire from politics for good—but Nixon was planning a comeback. He became a successful lawyer in New York. He campaigned for Republican candidates, thus building support for himself. In 1968, he announced that he would run for president again. His supporters said he was a "new Nixon," who was older, wiser, and more in control.

The election of 1968 came in the midst of turmoil and tragedy. Protests over the Vietnam War convinced President Lyndon Johnson not to run for reelection. Civil rights leader Martin Luther King Jr. was assassinated, sparking riots in many cities. Two months later, Democratic candidate for president Robert Kennedy was shot and killed. Furthermore, the Democratic Party was deeply split over the war and civil rights issues.

DEMOCRATIC PRANKS

Nixon had been the target of several campaign tricks during his political career. Many were the doing of Dick Tuck, a Democratic political worker who used pranks to upset Nixon or make him look bad. One trick came the day after the first televised presidential debate in the 1960 election. Tuck paid an elderly woman to approach Nixon and tell him he should not feel bad about losing the debate.

In the midst of this turmoil, Nixon tried to appeal to the silent majority—hard-working, law-abiding people who were bothered by the protests and riots. He promised to bring law and order to the country and peace with honor in Vietnam. In one of the closest U.S. presidential elections in history, Nixon narrowly defeated Hubert H. Humphrey, the vice president of the United States.

Richard Nixon won an easy victory in electoral votes in the 1968 presidential election, but he won less than 43 percent of the popular vote.

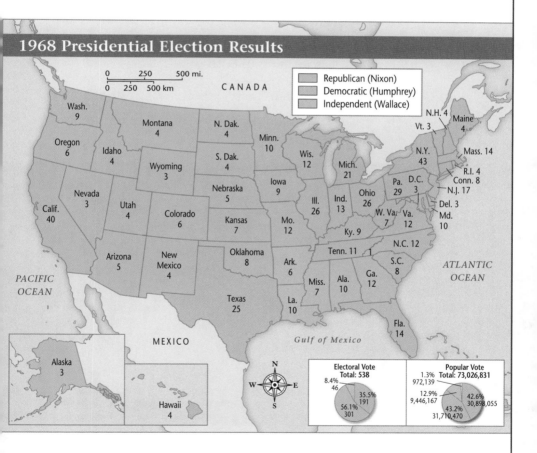

1968 Presidential Election Results

0   250   500 mi.
0   250   500 km

CANADA

Republican (Nixon)
Democratic (Humphrey)
Independent (Wallace)

Wash. 9
Montana 4
N. Dak. 4
Minn. 10
N.H. 4
Vt. 3
Maine 4

Oregon 6
Idaho 4
Wyoming 3
S. Dak. 4
Wis. 12
Mich. 21
N.Y. 43
Mass. 14
R.I. 4
Conn. 8

Nevada 3
Utah 4
Colorado 6
Nebraska 5
Iowa 9
Ill. 26
Ind. 13
Ohio 26
Pa. 29
D.C. 3
N.J. 17
Del. 3

Calif. 40
Kansas 7
Mo. 12
Ky. 9
W. Va. 7
Va. 12
Md. 10

Arizona 5
New Mexico 4
Oklahoma 8
Ark. 6
Tenn. 11
N.C. 12
S.C. 8

PACIFIC OCEAN

Texas 25
La. 10
Miss. 7
Ala. 10
Ga. 12

ATLANTIC OCEAN

MEXICO

Gulf of Mexico

Fla. 14

Alaska 3

Hawaii 4

N
W   E
S

Electoral Vote
Total: 538
8.4% 46
35.5% 191
56.1% 301

Popular Vote
Total: 73,026,831
1.3% 972,139
12.9% 9,446,167
42.6% 30,898,055
43.2% 31,710,470

In his first term, Nixon enjoyed two triumphs in foreign policy. He secretly sent National Security Adviser Henry Kissinger to open talks with the leaders of communist China and stunned the world when he announced that he himself would visit the country. This marked a major shift in U.S. policy: No American government had talked directly with the communists after they took control of China in 1949. Three months after that historic February 1972 visit, Nixon also visited the communist Soviet Union, signing a trade agreement and a treaty to limit nuclear weapons in both countries.

Nixon's Vietnam policy showed less striking results. In 1969, he had begun withdrawing American troops to turn over more of the fighting

to the army of South Vietnam. Early in 1970, Nixon sent troops into neighboring Cambodia to try to shut down supply routes used by North Vietnam. In the United States and elsewhere, antiwar protests surged once again. By early 1972, Nixon had cut troop strength in Vietnam to fewer than 70,000 soldiers. Still, the Vietnam War continued to rage, and peace talks seemed to be making no progress.

TRAGIC PROTESTS

Two of the protests over the Cambodia invasion ended in tragedy. At Kent State University in Ohio, nervous National Guard troops fired on a crowd of protesters, killing four students and wounding nine more. Ten days later, on May 14, 1970, a protest at Jackson State College in Mississippi was met by gunfire. Two students were killed and 12 were wounded. The shootings increased the fear and anger that many people in the antiwar movement felt toward the U.S. government.

National Guard troops fired tear gas to break up a crowd at Kent State University in Ohio on May 4, 1970. Seconds later, they shot four of the protesters dead.

21

Other issues also divided the United States at that time. One was busing. African-Americans had brought lawsuits against several school districts across the country. They argued that the existence of mostly black inner-city schools and mostly white suburban schools was a matter of school segregation, which the U.S. Supreme Court had banned in 1954. Several federal judges, hearing these arguments, agreed. They ordered school systems to bus black students from the cities to suburban schools and white suburban students into the cities. But many white people across the country objected.

Another issue dividing Americans was the growing movement for women's rights. Leaders of the movement were pushing for an amendment to the U.S. Constitution, known as the Equal Rights Amendment, which would guarantee equal rights for women. Some people—women as well as men—opposed this amendment for a number of reasons.

While Americans debated these issues, Nixon was preparing for his reelection campaign. He remembered how small his margin of victory had been in the 1968 election and hoped to use these issues, and others, to build support. When openings for federal judges arose, he chose conservatives who would be unlikely to vote for busing or women's rights. Meanwhile, he sent Vice President Spiro Agnew to speak across the country. Agnew blasted protesters, intellectuals, and the media. All of them, he implied, were less interested in the nation's success than in criticizing the government. His strongly worded attacks persuaded many Americans that the president and vice president shared their views.

Vice President Spiro Agnew became popular with many Americans when he criticized the television networks for presenting only negative news about the Vietnam War and Nixon administration actions.

Unbeknownst to the public, Nixon aides discussed ways to learn more about the government's critics and undermine their positions. In June 1970, Tom Huston, a young White House aide, developed a plan to use the FBI and CIA to get more intelligence on protest groups. He wanted agents to carry out break-ins in the offices of suspected groups. Huston warned the president of the legal problems with the plan:

> *Use of this technique is clearly illegal; it amounts to burglary. It is also highly risky and could result in great embarrassment if exposed. However, it is also the most fruitful tool and can produce the type of intelligence which cannot be obtained in any other fashion.*

Though these break-ins would be illegal, Nixon approved them. Only when FBI Director J. Edgar Hoover said he would not cooperate was the Huston Plan rejected.

Nixon's fury against critics and the media increased in 1971. On June 13, *The New York Times* began publishing documents that had been assembled in the Pentagon, headquarters of the Department of Defense. These Pentagon Papers traced U.S. policy during the Vietnam

THE "ENEMIES LIST"

Nixon's aides tried to find ways to punish those who opposed the president. On January 25, 1971, Tom Huston wrote a memo listing people who were not friendly to the administration. This enemies list was later expanded to include hundreds of people. Its purpose, a White House memo stated, was to identify Nixon opponents so staffers could use parts of the federal government to attack them.

War before Nixon became president. The papers showed that the government had not told the truth about the war to the American people. Though not damaged by the papers himself, Nixon was enraged that these top-secret documents had been leaked to the newspaper.

The Nixon administration tried using the courts to stop *The New York Times* and other newspapers from publishing the documents. In the end, the U.S. Supreme Court ruled against the administration, however.

Soon it became clear that the leaks had come from Daniel Ellsberg, a military analyst who worked under Henry Kissinger. Ellsberg had come to believe that the Vietnam War was a mistake, and he wanted people to know the truth about how the United States had entered the war. The papers revealed that officials of the Johnson administration had not always told the truth to the American people about the situation in Vietnam and its plans for the war. Nixon insisted that his people needed to do something to stop leaks. He delivered the message with brutal clarity to Charles Colson, a lawyer who worked in the White House. Nixon said:

> *Do whatever has to be done to stop these leaks and prevent further unauthorized disclosures; I don't want to be told why it can't be done ... I don't want excuses; I want results. I want it done, whatever the cost.*

25

In early July 1971, Colson hired E. Howard Hunt, a former CIA agent, as a White House consultant. Hunt's job was to find information on Ellsberg that could be used to damage his reputation. At the same time, John Ehrlichman, another top Nixon adviser,

Daniel Ellsberg later testified to a committee of the U.S. Senate about Nixon administration efforts to attack him.

was forming a group charged with learning more about Ellsberg. G. Gordon Liddy and Hunt were assigned to that group. Soon, the new unit had a name. They were called the Plumbers unit because their job was to plug leaks.

Liddy and Hunt decided to break into the offices of Ellsberg's psychiatrist in Los Angeles. They planned to photograph the doctor's files on Ellsberg and use the information to discredit him. They used Bernard Barker and some of the others who later carried out the Watergate break-in to do the job. But the burglary was completely botched. The burglars had to break open the door to get in, which meant that the burglary would be discovered. Worse, they found no files on Ellsberg in the office.

Nixon aides who were worried about national security had themselves committed a crime. They had also completely failed in their mission. In these ways, this burglary foreshadowed the Watergate break-in that would occur the following year. ◣

The 1972 Campaign

Chapter

3

While some of Nixon's aides were busy plugging leaks, many were also trying to help him win reelection. Some plans addressed how to pay tribute to the president at the Republican National Convention. With several nights of television coverage, the event offered the chance to reach millions of people.

Other plans aimed at trying to learn about the people hoping to be chosen as the Democratic candidate for president. Four candidates were the leading contenders. Senator Hubert Humphrey of Minnesota had been vice president under Lyndon Johnson and the Democratic nominee in 1968. Senator Edmund Muskie of Maine was a respected member of the Senate who had been the Democratic Party's candidate for vice president in 1968. Governor George Wallace of

Alabama had done well as a third-party candidate in 1968 running on a segregationist platform. He threatened to challenge Nixon's effort to win votes in the South. And finally, Senator George McGovern of South Dakota, a longtime opponent of the Vietnam War, was the peace candidate.

Lurking in the background was a fifth important candidate, Senator Edward (Ted) Kennedy of Massachusetts. Kennedy's brother John had beaten Nixon in the 1960 presidential election. Shot down by an assassin's bullet in 1963, President John F. Kennedy was admired by many. Their brother Robert had also shown great political strength until he, too, was assassinated. Nixon's team feared that Edward Kennedy could take advantage of his brothers' popularity—and his own speaking skill—to mount a strong campaign.

Senator George McGovern started criticizing U.S. involvement in Vietnam in 1963.

Nixon and his people hoped that McGovern would be named the Democratic candidate. They felt that his liberal voting record in the Senate and his strong positions against the Vietnam War could be used against him.

They got their wish. In January 1971, Kennedy—who was worried about a personal scandal—chose not to run. Muskie pulled out in the spring after poor results in early Democratic elections held in different states. Wallace was shot while campaigning in Maryland in May 1972. Because he was seriously wounded, he had to withdraw from the race. Humphrey campaigned hard, but he trailed McGovern in delegates at the National Convention. McGovern, who had a good campaign organization and whose message appealed to many Democrats, would become the Democratic Party candidate.

Nixon had numerous advantages in the run for the presidency. He could use the trappings of the office to

MUSKIE'S DOWNFALL

Edmund Muskie's campaign started to fail just before New Hampshire Democrats voted for the candidate they wanted. A local newspaper published a letter supposedly written by a Muskie campaign worker. According to the letter, the senator had insulted African-Americans as well as French Canadians—many of whom lived in New Hampshire. In fact, the letter had been written by a Nixon aide. The paper also repeated a rumor about inappropriate behavior by Muskie's wife. The next day, Muskie stood in front of the paper's offices to protest the stories. He was highly emotional, and reports said that he cried. That damaged his image as a calm, capable leader and perhaps cost him votes in New Hampshire and other states.

impress voters with his authority. He could also spend government money on new projects to help win support in key areas. His triumphant trips to China and the Soviet Union early in 1972 were fresh in voters' minds. And he had a huge amount of money to spend on the campaign. Under rules in force until April 7, 1972, the Nixon team could raise money without recording who had given it, which made it easier to persuade people to donate money. With a strong effort, Nixon's campaign raised more than $20 million in early 1972. About $1.8 million of that money was in cash. That cash came to play a role in the Watergate scandal.

As the Nixon campaign was getting under way late in 1971, however, the Democratic candidate was still undecided. A group of Nixon advisers talked about ways to gather intelligence on the various candidates. They also talked about dirty tricks that could be played on Democrats.

Three White House aides played key roles in the Committee to Re-elect the President (CREEP)—H.R. Haldeman, John Ehrlichman, and John Dean. Haldeman was the president's chief of staff—the person who decided who got to see Nixon, how issues were presented to the president, and, often, who should carry out the president's decisions. Ehrlichman advised Nixon on policy issues. Dean was the White House counsel, the lawyer to the president.

SELECTED LIST OF NIXON AIDES IN 1971

Name	Job Title	Links with Others	Responsibilities
H.R. Haldeman	Chief of staff (White House)	Very close to Nixon	Supervised all other White House workers; controlled who got to see Nixon; helped plan campaign strategy
John Ehrlichman	Chief domestic policy adviser (White House)	Very close to Nixon	Gave advice on domestic issues and politics, including campaign strategy
Henry Kissinger	Chief national security adviser (White House)	Very close to Nixon	Gave advice on foreign policy
John Dean	President's counsel (White House)	Worked closely with others	Gave legal advice to president and staff
Charles Colson	Liaison with special interest groups (White House)	Liked by Nixon for toughness	Developed relations with business groups; advised on political matters
G. Gordon Liddy	Adviser on domestic policy (White House); counsel (CREEP)	Hired by Mitchell	Planned Plumbers' work; at CREEP, developed plan for getting political information
E. Howard Hunt	Consultant (White House)	Hired by Colson	Gathered information to be used against political enemies
John Mitchell	Attorney general (Cabinet); campaign director (CREEP)	Very close to Nixon	As attorney general supervised Justice Department and FBI; for CREEP, ran campaign
Jeb Magruder	Deputy director (CREEP)	Had worked under Haldeman	Ran campaign until Mitchell took over

Nixon wanted his trusted friend John Mitchell to be in charge of his reelection committee. But Mitchell was serving as attorney general, so Jeb Stuart Magruder ran CREEP instead. Still, Mitchell played a central role in making campaign decisions, even while he was attorney general. Mitchell finally left that job and took over as full-time director of CREEP on March 1, 1972, and Magruder became his deputy.

In December 1971, G. Gordon Liddy had been brought to CREEP to work as counsel, or the group's lawyer. He was also told that he would be in charge of efforts to gather intelligence and disrupt the Democratic candidates. Liddy later described how he saw his job:

> *I knew exactly what had to be done and why, and I was under no illusion about its legality. Although spies in the enemy camp and electronic surveillance were nothing new in American presidential politics, we were going to go beyond that. As far as I was concerned, anything went.*

Liddy presented his plans to Mitchell, Dean, and several other officials. Mitchell balked when Liddy asked for $1 million to pay for the effort. He told Liddy to revise his plans to include fewer missions and to cut the cost in half—but never said anything about cutting out illegal activities. A $250,000 plan that included phone bugs was finally approved on March 30, 1972. This was the seed of the Watergate break-in.

Digging up the Story

Chapter

4

The main feature of Liddy's plan was to break into the headquarters of the Democratic National Committee (DNC) at the Watergate complex in Washington, D.C. The idea was to plant bugs on telephones in the DNC offices and photograph documents there. Liddy hoped that these actions would yield information that could be used against the Democrats.

To do the work, Liddy turned to E. Howard Hunt, his partner in the break-in of the offices of Daniel Ellsberg's psychiatrist. They added James McCord, Bernard Barker, and three others to carry out the break-in, plus Alfred Baldwin to act as a lookout. Unfortunately for the Nixon team, the five burglars were discovered by the police and arrested early in the morning of June 17, 1972.

Liddy's plan collapsed when the Watergate burglars were arrested. When the arrests took place, Hunt contacted Jeb Magruder, the second-in-command at CREEP. Magruder was shocked that the team had used James McCord, CREEP's security chief, to take part in the break-in. Once the police realized who McCord was, Magruder knew that CREEP would be linked to the crime. He quickly told John Mitchell and two other top officials. Magruder later described the way they were thinking that day:

> *At some point that Saturday morning I realized that this was not just hard-nosed politics, this was a crime that could destroy us all. The cover-up, thus, was immediate and automatic; no one ever considered that there would not be a cover-up.*

Someone decided that CREEP should try contacting Richard Kleindienst, who had replaced John Mitchell as attorney general. The idea was for Kleindienst to tell the police to let McCord go. Kleindienst exploded in outrage at this suggestion. He knew that such a move would be obstruction of justice—the crime of taking steps to block an investigation. He refused.

The day the arrests took place, Nixon was enjoying a vacation in Florida. The next day, Charles Colson, the White House worker who had hired Hunt, told Nixon of the break-in. Colson did not tell Nixon that Hunt was involved, however.

White House Consultant Tied to Bugging Figur

Newspaper reports in The Washington Post *brought details of Watergate to the public while official investigations took place behind the scenes.*

The Monday after the arrests—June 19—others began to take control of and destroy evidence. White House counsel John Dean knew that evidence of the involvement of people who worked in the White House in the break-in could be found in Hunt's White House office. He took everything out of the safe in Hunt's office in case investigators went there. Mitchell told Magruder to burn his file about Liddy's plan, which Magruder did in his home fireplace that same night.

Reporters were busy, too. On the morning of June 20, *The Washington Post* revealed that the burglars carried an address book containing the name of Howard Hunt and his White House phone number. Within just three days of the break-in, connections to CREEP and the White House had become public.

On June 20, Nixon returned from his vacation. His chief of staff, H.R. Haldeman, told him many details about the break-in and made it clear that CREEP and White House staffers were involved. Though Colson had already told Nixon that the break-in and arrests had taken place, this was the first time that Nixon definitely knew that people who worked for him were involved. This much is known from a tape recording made of the conversation. Unfortunately, some details of the conversation were lost.

Two days later, Nixon made his first public statement on Watergate. He denied any White House involvement and, since it was a criminal matter, said he would not discuss it further.

OFFICIAL ROLES OF THE FBI AND CIA

The main task of the FBI is to investigate actions that break federal law and arrest those responsible. The FBI also has an intelligence function. Agents investigate and track individuals and groups thought to be threats to the nation's security. The CIA's main task is to carry out intelligence in other countries. At the time of Watergate, the CIA was not supposed to gather intelligence within the United States. It did not always follow that rule, however.

The next day, June 23, Nixon and Haldeman had a crucial conversation. Haldeman reported what Nixon's aides had learned about the FBI investigation and how they thought they should proceed:

John Dean ... concurs now with Mitchell's recommendation that the only way to solve this ... is for us to have [CIA Deputy Director Vernon] Walters call [Acting FBI Director] Pat Gray and just say, "Stay ... out of this ... this is business here; we don't want you to go any further on it."

Nixon's aides hoped that Gray would believe that the break-in was part of a CIA operation that needed to remain secret to protect the nation.

That, of course, was a lie. Not only that, but the attempt to stop the investigation was obstruction of justice—a crime. Nixon agreed to the plan anyway. In writing his memoir, *RN*, Nixon explained how he saw Watergate, which clarifies why he went along with this plan:

> *My reaction to the Watergate break-in was completely pragmatic. If it was also cynical, it was a cynicism born of experience. I had been in politics too long, and seen everything from dirty tricks to vote fraud. I could not muster much moral outrage over a political bugging.*

Other efforts were being made to cover up the involvement of Nixon's aides. White House Counsel John Dean talked to Acting FBI Director L. Patrick Gray, who controlled the investigation.

L. Patrick Gray was loyal to Nixon and determined to help the president in any way he could. This led him to make several poor decisions.

Dean convinced Gray to allow him to sit in on all interviews the FBI had with White House workers. He also got Gray to agree to send him copies of FBI interview reports. With these agreements— which should never have been made—Dean could closely follow the investigation.

Gray then made an even more serious error of judgment. On June 28, Dean gave Gray two envelopes of material that he had taken from the safe in Howard Hunt's White House office. These had to do with Hunt's efforts to gather political dirt on Democrats. The material was, Dean said, political dynamite. Gray held onto the material for several months. He never said anything about it to FBI agents. Later in the year, he burned it.

By the end of June 1972, the FBI had identified G. Gordon Liddy as a suspect and tracked him down to CREEP's offices. Although Liddy refused to talk, the White House worried that the trail would lead to John Mitchell, who had hired Liddy. Soon after Liddy became a suspect, a surprising announcement hit the news: John Mitchell was going to resign as head of CREEP. The reason given was family matters, but the real reason was that Nixon feared the investigation would soon lead to Mitchell. Nixon wanted Mitchell as far removed from him as possible. Mitchell, loyal to the president, agreed to resign.

At the same time the FBI was investigating those suspected of being involved in the break-in, several newspapers were also breaking important stories about Watergate. Two young reporters for *The Washington Post* wrote many of these stories. Bob Woodward and Carl Bernstein had been accidentally thrown together on the story on the weekend of the arrests. They quickly became a team—known as Woodstein. They worked together extremely well despite the fact they had very different working styles. What they shared was dogged determination and good sources.

One of those sources was a high-placed government official nicknamed Deep Throat. Only the reporters and a few others knew the identity of this source. From time to time, Deep Throat met secretly with *The Washington Post* reporter Bob Woodward in a parking garage. At those

THE SECRET OF DEEP THROAT

The identity of Deep Throat was a secret until 2005. That year, Deep Throat was identified as W. Mark Felt, an assistant director of the FBI during Watergate. He had met Bob Woodward in 1969 or 1970, and the two had become friends. A long-time member of the FBI, Felt was fiercely loyal to the bureau and resented the pressure the Nixon White House put on it. He may also have been angered when L. Patrick Gray, and not he, was named to replace J. Edgar Hoover as director when Hoover died in May 1972. Though Felt was not a part of the FBI teams of investigators looking into Watergate, he had access to reports from those teams because he had such a high position in the organization. Woodward and Bernstein had vowed to keep his identity secret until he died. Felt's family, who wanted him to have the credit, revealed his role in 2005.

meetings, Deep Throat commented on the accuracy of story ideas the pair was developing and occasionally suggested the reporters look in certain directions.

While FBI agents were carrying out their investigation of Watergate—and while reporters like Woodward and Bernstein were trying to dig out the truth—members of the Nixon administration undertook new efforts to make sure the cover-up would work. Dean brought in Herbert Kalmbach, Nixon's personal lawyer and a skilled fund-raiser. He asked Kalmbach to raise $50,000 to $100,000 that could be used to pay the burglars and their families. The cash was meant as hush money—or money to buy their silence. This, too, was a matter of obstructing justice. By September, Kalmbach was having second thoughts and dropped out of the arrangement. This slowed down the payments, which angered the burglars.

Carl Bernstein (second from left) and Bob Woodward (center) worked together at The Washington Post with publisher Katharine Graham (far left), managing editor Howard Simons (second from right), and executive editor Ben Bradlee.

On July 5, 1972, a grand jury first began meeting to hear evidence about the Watergate break-in. A few days later, the investigators made a breakthrough. Baldwin—the lookout from the hotel that was across the street—agreed to cooperate with government investigators in return for not being prosecuted. He linked Hunt and Liddy to the break-in.

On September 15, the grand jury announced its decisions. It handed down indictments, or formal criminal charges, against McCord, Barker, Gonzalez, Martinez, Sturgis, Hunt, and Liddy. It charged them with burglary and illegal wiretapping. Over the next few months, investigators continued to piece together evidence that linked Liddy and Hunt to the Watergate break-in.

WHAT GRAND JURIES DO

Grand juries meet in secret and hear evidence brought by prosecutors. Then they decide if enough evidence exists to indict someone for committing a crime. Being indicted is being formally accused of a crime. An indictment does not mean that a person is guilty. It only means there is enough evidence that the person may have committed a crime. Guilt or innocence is decided in a full jury trial.

Less than two months after the indictments, the nation went to the polls. Richard Nixon defeated George McGovern in the popular vote by an overwhelming margin, receiving 60 percent to McGovern's 39 percent. Nixon convincingly won 49 of the 50 states, giving him 520 of the electoral votes to just 17 won by McGovern.

WATERGATE SCANDAL

Kleindienst

Haldeman

Ehrlichman

Magruder

Gray

Dean

But while Nixon and his aides were celebrating the president's reelection, the Watergate burglars were losing patience. Hunt called Colson—who had originally hired him and who worked in the White House—after the election and told him that the burglars' lawyers had not yet received all the money they needed. Their own families were not being cared for financially either. He pointed out that the burglars were hiding the truth about people higher up, but that they expected to be protected, too. Hunt also wrote a memorandum to another Nixon worker repeating this message. The phone call and memorandum had an effect. Haldeman authorized sending the burglars $350,000 out of a secret cash fund he controlled. ◣

Haldeman, Ehrlichman, Magruder, and Dean – along with President Nixon himself – were actively involved in the Watergate cover-up. Acting FBI Director Gray cooperated with the Nixon team. Attorney General Kleindienst tried to oversee a fair investigation while at the same time keeping the president informed of political dangers he faced.

43

New Facts Come Out

Chapter

5

R ichard Nixon enjoyed two triumphs early in 1973. On January 20, he was sworn in as president for the second time. Then, just one week later came another step toward peace in Vietnam. After months of negotiation, diplomats signed a peace pact in Paris, France, that called for the end of fighting in Vietnam. In the wake of the peace agreement, polls showed that nearly 70 percent of the American people approved of the job Nixon was doing as president.

Just days before Nixon took the oath of office, the trial of the burglars opened in the courthouse of Judge John Sirica. The U.S. District Court judge had a reputation for being tough. Hunt, Barker, Gonzalez, Martinez, and Sturgis all pleaded guilty. Since McCord and Liddy pleaded not guilty, their cases had gone to trial.

But Nixon could not bask in the celebratory mood of his inauguration or the surge in popularity. The shadow of Watergate still dogged him and his presidency. On either side of these two achievements were new developments in the investigation into Watergate. Those developments would eventually lead to the unraveling of the cover-up—and to the end of Richard Nixon's presidency. Though it began well for Nixon, 1973 would prove to be a long and difficult year for him.

Richard Nixon (far left) took the oath of office from Chief Justice of the Supreme Court Warren Burger (far right) in 1973, while wife Pat Nixon looked on.

45

Judge Sirica, a Republican, had been named to the U.S. District Court by President Dwight D. Eisenhower.

On January 30, 1973, the jury found McCord and Liddy guilty. But Judge Sirica was not entirely satisfied. He scolded the prosecutors for not getting more information out of the defendants. He was convinced that all the facts were not yet known.

Sirica would set the sentences for the seven men. Hoping they would finally break and begin to tell the truth, he delayed setting their sentences for several weeks. That was an important step in uncovering the cover-up.

Three weeks later, on February 7, the Senate voted unanimously to set up a special committee to investigate the Watergate break-in and related issues. The committee would have four Democratic members and three Republicans.

Nixon met with Chief of Staff H.R. Haldeman, Domestic Policy Adviser John Ehrlichman, and Counsel John Dean to discuss how to handle the committee. They agreed to pretend to cooperate with the Senate committee but act behind the scenes to block its work.

On February 23, Nixon asked Ehrlichman about the degree to which he, Haldeman, Mitchell, and Colson were involved in Watergate. The president also discussed ways witnesses could say things to prevent them from either admitting guilt or committing perjury. Nixon also vowed that he would not let any of his aides go to jail.

JOHN SIRICA (1904–1992)

After graduating from Georgetown University's law school in 1926, John Sirica worked as a lawyer in private practice for nearly 30 years. He became a judge in the U.S. District Court for the District of Columbia in 1957. There, he earned the nickname Maximum John for handing out tough sentences. Sirica was also a controversial judge; a larger-than-usual share of his decisions were overturned in courts of appeals. In April 1971, he became the chief judge in his district court. When the Watergate break-in case reached the court, he assigned himself to it. Sirica retired in 1986 and died six years later at age 88.

47

In making this vow, Nixon was raising the possibility of granting the burglars a presidential pardon, which would excuse them from serving any time in jail. The president was, in effect, suggesting a deal that would save both the burglars and his presidency. As long as they protected him and his aides by refusing to tell Sirica any more, he would protect them by pardoning them. These conversations show that Nixon knew a great deal about the Watergate mess and that he was intent on covering up the facts.

On February 17, Nixon took a step that turned out to be a huge mistake. L. Patrick Gray was only the temporary FBI director until a permanent one was named. Nixon decided to reward Gray for his loyalty by appointing him permanent director. In order to take that position, though, Gray had to be confirmed by the Senate. First, the Senate Judiciary Committee would question Gray—and the Watergate investigation would be high on their list of questions.

Gray's testimony to the Senate Judiciary Committee proved to be very damaging. On February 28, he revealed that he had given John Dean, the president's counsel, copies of the reports FBI agents had made when questioning people. He also told the committee that Dean had sat in on FBI interviews with White House staffers. These actions had been inappropriate, and Gray's revealing them was a bombshell.

The next problem for the White House arose in Judge Sirica's courtroom, where the date for sentencing burglars Liddy and Hunt was nearing. Sirica had delayed sentencing in the hopes that one or more of the burglars would decide to cooperate with prosecutors in exchange for a lighter sentence. His plan paid off. Unwilling to go to jail, burglar James McCord decided to end his silence, giving prosecutors a major breakthrough.

The testimony of L. Patrick Gray (left) led the Senate Judiciary Committee to demand that John Dean appear as a witness, but President Nixon refused to allow it, raising tensions between him and Congress.

49

McCord was ready to tell the judge what he knew in order to receive a lighter sentence. On March 19, the day before sentencing, he hand-delivered a letter to the judge. Sirica read it aloud in the courtroom the next day. It included several charges:

James McCord (center) did not speak to reporters outside a Washington, D.C., courtroom in March 1973; his lawyer Bernard Fensterwald (right) handled the questions.

> *1. There was political pressure applied to the defendants to plead guilty and remain silent.*

2. Perjury occurred during the trial in matters highly material to the very structure, orientation, and impact of the government's case, and to the motivation and intent of the defendants.

3. Others involved in the Watergate operation were not identified during the trial, when they could have been by those testifying.

While reporters rushed outside to write the story, Sam Dash, the chief lawyer on the Senate Watergate committee, stayed behind. He talked to McCord, who told him that Jeb Magruder, the deputy director of CREEP who testified at the burglars' trials, had perjured himself. McCord also said that White House counsel John Dean had been involved in the scandal.

The next day, President Nixon met with Dean. This meeting included several developments that later haunted Nixon. Dean began by updating Nixon on the status of the investigation. He warned the president of the growing problem, which he called a cancer close to the presidency. He warned Nixon that his aides might begin committing perjury to avoid being convicted of a crime.

WHITE HOUSE COUNSEL

The White House counsel has two main responsibilities. One is to advise the president on legal issues that arise from policies and decisions. The other is to protect the constitutional powers of the office of the presidency. Counsels review proposed laws, take part in planning meetings, and discuss the appointment of federal judges. Presidents must place a huge amount of trust in their counsels. As a result, some name friends to the post, though that was not the case with John Dean.

Dean told the president that Hunt was holding out for more money and suggested that the cost might run as high as $1 million. Nixon responded by saying:

> *You could get a million dollars. And you could get it in cash. I, I know where it could be gotten.*

In the spring of 1973, John Dean was quite worried about the unraveling cover-up, but he put on a cheerful front.

In other words, the president was agreeing to pay to keep them quiet.

The next day, in a meeting with Mitchell and others, Nixon made another statement that would come to haunt him. He told his aides to make sure the burglars did not talk. Later, Nixon's words were used as evidence of his knowledge of and participation in the cover-up.

Nixon asked Dean to prepare a report for him on Watergate, spelling out who knew what and when. This worried Dean. He was clearly involved in the cover-up, and various people could testify to that effect. Nixon could use the report to protect himself, though, claiming that he did not know various facts until he had received them from Dean or others. Dean began working on the report, but he worked slowly. On March 30, Dean, feeling threatened, got a lawyer for himself. He was now more worried about his own survival than about protecting the president. Dean's lawyer set up a meeting with the prosecutor, and Dean began telling them what he knew. He hoped that in return for his information, they would grant him immunity from any prosecution.

Dean insisted on a key ground rule for his conversations with prosecutors. He would talk only if they promised not to reveal his cooperation to top officials in the Justice Department. He was certain that if those officials learned of his cooperation, they would tell the president, who would then move against him. Dean's fears turned out to be justified.

In mid-April 1973, the president's two close advisers, H.R. Haldeman and John Ehrlichman, began to worry about whether they could count on Dean to keep quiet. They were concerned about Hunt also. Ehrlichman had heard that Hunt was ready to talk to prosecutors. Hunt would describe not only the Watergate break-in but also the burglary of Ellsberg's psychiatrist's office, and he would link Mitchell and Ehrlichman to that crime. Finally, Hunt would talk about the hush money, which would link Dean and others to obstruction of justice charges.

CREEP's deputy director, Jeb Magruder, was talking to prosecutors as well, and his statements matched much of what Dean had said. Early on the morning of Sunday, April 15, the prosecutors met with Attorney General Richard Kleindienst. They explained that from Dean and Magruder, they knew that John Mitchell, the former attorney general, was involved in the meetings discussing Liddy's plans for intelligence gathering, which had led to the Watergate break-in. They also knew about Haldeman and Ehrlichman taking part in the hush money effort. That afternoon, Kleindienst told Nixon that Mitchell, Haldeman, and Ehrlichman were likely to be charged with crimes. Nixon had expected this in Mitchell's case but was shocked that his two closest advisers were vulnerable. He was also surprised to learn that it was Dean who was providing prosecutors with information.

That night, Nixon told Haldeman and Ehrlichman what he had heard. The next day, he met with Dean—without telling him that he knew Dean was cooperating. The president suggested that Dean resign over his involvement in Watergate. Dean refused unless Haldeman and Ehrlichman did so also. Nixon, reluctant to lose his two closest aides, did not press him.

Nixon met continually with John Ehrlichman (right), one of his two closest and most trusted aides.

On April 17, 1973, Nixon made a public statement on Watergate. First, he announced that he had agreed to let his staffers testify before the Senate Watergate committee. This reversed the earlier White House position. He also announced that he thought nobody from the administration should be given immunity from prosecution. This was aimed directly at Dean, who wanted immunity.

The situation was getting worse for the Nixon administration. On April 27, *The Washington Post* and other papers reported that L. Patrick Gray had destroyed files he had been given by Dean. These were the files from Hunt's safe, which Dean had told Gray were political dynamite. That the acting director of the FBI would destroy evidence was too much. Reacting to the public outrage over his actions, Gray resigned.

More resignations were to come. The growing stories about the involvement of Haldeman and Ehrlichman forced Nixon to let them go. On April 30, Nixon spoke in a televised address to the

THE ELLSBERG CASE

John Dean told prosecutors about the break-in of Daniel Ellsberg's psychiatrist's office. Ellsberg was being tried in California for revealing government secrets, and the information about the break-in had to be revealed to the judge handling that case. Soon after, it also came out that Ellsberg's phone had been illegally wiretapped. A month later, the judge dismissed the case on the grounds that Ellsberg could not be given a fair trial because of these illegal actions by government officials. Later, Ehrlichman and the Plumbers were convicted of violating civil rights for ordering and carrying out the break-in.

nation. In it, he denied that he had known anything about the involvement of members of his administration in Watergate before March 1973.

Nixon claimed that, beginning on March 21, he had personally begun to look into the Watergate mess, determined to find out the truth no matter who was involved. He then revealed that Halde-man and Ehrlichman were both resigning. Nixon expressed his regrets, praising both men for their fine service. Nixon also announced the resignation of Dean, for whom he had no praise at all. Finally, he announced that Attorney General Kleindienst was resigning because he had had close relations with some of the people being investigated. Kleindienst, who had no connection to Watergate or the cover-up, was deeply disappointed at having his resignation announced with the others. ◣

Like many Watergate-related events, the four resignations on April 30, 1973, received banner headlines in the newspapers the following day.

57

Committee Hearings and Court Proceedings

Chapter

6

During the spring of 1973, while prosecutors were investigating Watergate, another investigation was taking place in Congress. In early February, the Senate had voted to form a special committee to investigate the Watergate affair. The chair of the Senate committee was Senator Sam Ervin, a Democrat from North Carolina. The leading Republican member was Senator Howard Baker of Tennessee.

The committee had three other Democrats and two other Republicans as members. Supporting these senators was a staff of more than 150 people. This large team included lawyers, investigators, consultants, and secretaries. Leading this team were Sam Dash, counsel to the Democratic majority, and Fred Thompson, counsel to the Republican minority.

Committee staffers had been interviewing possible witnesses during the spring. The senators agreed to give John Dean immunity from prosecution for anything he said to the committee. Prosecutors could still try him on the basis of other evidence, but they could not use his words to the committee against him. This was a key decision, because Dean knew a lot about the cover-up, and immunity gave him the freedom to tell his story completely and without hesitation.

The Senate Watergate committee included, from the left, Republicans Lowell Weicker, Edward Gurney, counsel Fred Thompson, and Howard Baker, plus Democrats Sam Ervin, counsel Sam Dash, Herman Talmadge, Daniel Inouye, and Joseph Montoya.

Public Senate hearings began on May 17, 1973. Leaks of what key witnesses would say had appeared in several newspapers in the weeks leading up to the hearings. The prospect of seeing Mitchell, Dean, Haldeman, and Ehrlichman talk convinced television networks to broadcast the hearings. When advertisers objected to all three networks canceling regular programming, the networks agreed to take turns showing the committee and run their normal shows on the off days. Though the hearings took place during the day, millions watched.

At first, much of the testimony was dry and dull, full of references to memos and meetings at specific dates and times. Some witnesses were called simply to explain the organization of CREEP. Still, some damaging charges were made from the start.

THE AMERICAN PUBLIC AND WATERGATE

Until the Senate Watergate hearings, the American people paid little attention to the scandal. Up to that point, much of the story took place behind the scenes in private meetings of Nixon aides or investigators. Newspaper stories that included charges against various members of the Nixon team did not cause great public outcry. Some Americans believed that journalists were trying to undermine the president—a president whose popularity rose sharply in January 1973 because of the end of the Vietnam War. Most people saw the Watergate affair as an isolated incident and believed the president when he said he had no involvement. The televised Senate hearings brought the issue to the forefront of American political life. Watching people who worked for the president say that they had taken illegal actions— and that the president had done so as well—heightened people's interest in the Watergate scandal.

In the first week, James McCord testified that the burglars had been offered a presidential pardon before their trial if they would remain silent. In a pardon, a person accused or convicted of a crime is allowed to go free. This was important because only the president of the United States can pardon someone for a federal offense. McCord's statement was verified by a witness who had sometimes worked with Dean. Still, the committee could only link the offer to the president based on hearsay—what people had been told by someone else. Hearsay cannot be used as evidence in court.

The Nixon administration pushed Senator Baker (left) to try to end the hearings quickly, but he joined with Senator Ervin (center) to conduct a thorough investigation.

61

The next revelation, in the second week, came from Maurice Stans and Hugh Sloan. Both had handled the money side of the reelection campaign. Both said that John Mitchell had approved using CREEP campaign money to pay G. Gordon Liddy for the Watergate break-in.

Jeb Magruder charged that Mitchell had told him to go ahead with the break-in. He also linked others, including Charles Colson, the White House aide who had originally hired E. Howard Hunt, and John Dean, to the burglary.

For weeks in the summer of 1973, millions of Americans watched in fascination as witnesses like H.R. Haldeman testified about Watergate to the Senate committee.

Dean came before the committee starting on June 25 and was questioned for several days. Throughout the hearings, Senator Howard Baker said that the committee's task was to find out this crucial information:

> *What did the president know, and when did he know it?*

Dean, as the president's counsel, was in a good position to tell Baker what he wanted to know.

Dean gave strong testimony against Nixon. Even so, it was Dean's word against the president's. Dean told the committee about a September 15, 1972, meeting:

> *I left with the impression that the president was well aware of what had been going on regarding the success of keeping the White House out of the Watergate scandal, and I also had expressed to him my concern that I was not confident the cover-up could be maintained indefinitely.*

Other witnesses, however, supported the president. CREEP Director John Mitchell denied that he had approved the break-in and said that he worked hard to protect Nixon from any involvement in the cover-up. He explained that he thought it best to block the investigation of this crime because it would inevitably lead to the discovery of several other illegal actions committed by the White House.

On July 16, Alexander Butterfield, a staffer who worked under Haldeman, was called before the committee. In just half an hour, he gave the most significant piece of information to come out of the hearings. Butterfield revealed that the president had a secret tape-recording system. It recorded all of Nixon's conversations in his White House office as well as his telephone conversations.

Alexander Butterfield became a surprise witness at the Senate Watergate hearings.

This meant that Dean's charges against Nixon could be checked. The nation could learn what Nixon knew and when he knew it.

That night, Nixon, in a hospital bed with pneumonia, met with several advisers. Among them were Alexander Haig, who had replaced Haldeman as chief of staff, and Leonard Garment, Nixon's personal attorney. Several people urged Nixon to destroy the tapes. Garment pointed out that this would be destroying evidence. He said that such a step would lead to impeachment of the president. He also said that if the tapes were destroyed, he would resign.

The tapes quickly became the focus of the investigation. On July 18, the day after Butterfield mentioned them, the Senate committee asked Nixon to turn over the tapes. Nixon refused on the grounds of executive privilege, the principle that the president did not have to give Congress information about his private meetings with advisers. His statement added another reason:

> *[Though they are] entirely consistent with what I ... have stated to be the truth ... they contain comments that persons with different perspectives and motivations would inevitably interpret in different ways.*

The committee disagreed about the use of executive privilege. The senators voted to subpoena the tapes.

The hearings continued. John Ehrlichman staunchly defended the president. H.R. Haldeman did, too. He directly contradicted Dean's claim that on March 21, 1973, the president had agreed to raise more hush money for Hunt and the burglars. Nixon, Haldeman said, had told Dean that paying the money would be wrong. While Nixon had used those words in that conversation, they were not in relation to the hush money. Haldeman had to admit that he based this claim on having heard the tape of that conversation between Nixon and Dean. The idea that Nixon had let Haldeman listen to tapes while denying that right to Congress angered the senators even more.

While the committee hearings went on, another investigation was taking place. Nixon had named Elliot Richardson to replace Richard Kleindienst as attorney general. Acting on a promise made to the Senate, Richardson named a special prosecutor to investigate Watergate and prosecute

THE JOB OF SPECIAL PROSECUTORS

Prosecutors try to prove in court that a person accused of a crime is guilty. They work for the U.S. Department of Justice. Some cases involve possible crimes by members of the executive branch. In these cases, it is feared that the Justice Department can put pressure on prosecutors so they will not thoroughly pursue the case. That concern during Watergate led to the naming of a special prosecutor. In 1978, Congress passed a law that set rules for when a special prosecutor should be named and how that official could remain independent. The law was used several times during the 1980s and 1990s to investigate the actions of government officials. In 1999, the law expired and was not renewed.

anyone who had committed a crime. He appointed Archibald Cox, a professor from Harvard Law School, and gave him broad powers of investigation. He was given the authority to look beyond Watergate into any areas he thought appropriate. Importantly, only Richardson had the authority to fire Cox. Nixon fumed in private at the choice of Cox and his broad powers but publicly offered support.

In Senate hearings, Attorney General Elliot Richardson (right) promised to give special prosecutor Archibald Cox (left) a free hand to carry out his investigation. Cox vowed to use that freedom to get to the bottom of Watergate.

When Butterfield revealed the White House tape-recording system, Cox pounced on the opportunity the tapes offered to learn what the president had known. Like the Senate committee, he sent Nixon a request for the tapes. On July 23, Nixon refused to turn them over. Cox immediately went to Judge John Sirica, who had jurisdiction over Watergate-related matters. Sirica issued a subpoena for the tapes.

Once again, Nixon refused to turn them over. Cox and Sirica then called the Watergate grand jury into a public session. There, the 23 jurors agreed that the subpoena should be enforced.

Meanwhile, more problems arose for the Nixon administration. Nixon was being investigated over possible problems with his income tax returns, and even worse charges hit the vice president. Spiro Agnew was being investigated for taking bribes when he had been governor of Maryland. In October, Agnew agreed to accept the charges and pay a fine. He also resigned from office. By the end of the year, Agnew was replaced as vice president by Gerald R. Ford, a longtime member of the House of Representatives from Michigan.

In late summer, President Nixon had made another televised address about Watergate. In it, he defended his refusal to hand over the tapes. Then, a lawyer argued Nixon's case about not turning over the tapes to Judge Sirica, who denied the president's claim. But the judge offered a compromise— that the president give the tapes to him. He would listen

THE 25TH AMENDMENT

Gerald Ford became vice president because of the 25th Amendment to the Constitution. Until it was passed in 1967, the country had no way to replace a vice president if that office became vacant. To fix that problem, Congress passed and states ratified the 25th Amendment. It said that if the vice presidency became vacant, the president would name someone to the job. Then the Senate and House of Representatives would both have to vote to approve that person. Once that happened, the person could take office as vice president.

to them and turn over those that applied to the case. Neither Cox nor Nixon liked this idea, and they appealed. On October 12, the U.S. Court of Appeals ruled against Nixon and ordered him to turn over the tapes.

By this time, the president was even more determined not to release the tapes because he knew about a serious problem with them. In early October, he had told his secretary, Rose Mary Woods, to begin typing up summaries of the tapes. In the process, she discovered that two of the tapes requested by Cox did not exist.

Rose Mary Woods, Richard Nixon's secretary from 1951 until 1974, was so close to the Nixon family that one of the president's daughters called her Aunt Rose.

Nixon was certain that no one would believe this was an accident. Worse, the tape of Nixon talking to Haldeman back on June 20, 1972, now had a gap in it. Woods said that she had accidentally copied over part of the tape while taking a phone call. Again, Nixon knew that this would be seen as destruction of evidence.

Negotiations went on about the tapes. Nixon insisted on only providing summaries, while Cox insisted on the actual tapes. As days passed, Nixon became increasingly angry at Cox—and more determined to get rid of him. Finally, on October 20, 1973, Nixon demanded that Attorney General Richardson fire Cox. Richardson refused and resigned instead. His top deputy, William Ruckelshaus, also refused and resigned. Only the number-three man at the Justice Department agreed that the president had the authority to fire Cox. Robert Bork—the acting attorney general—fired Cox.

The next day, the newspapers called the two resignations and the firing of Cox the Saturday Night Massacre. Congress and the White House received thousands of letters and telegrams over the next few days. Many protested the president's actions. Newspapers joined the criticism. *The Salt Lake Tribune*, despite years of support for Nixon, said:

> *We now find it necessary, for the good of the country, to call upon Richard M. Nixon to resign.*

The court decision and firestorm of protest that greeted the firing of Cox forced Nixon to make concessions. To comply with the order of the court of appeals, he agreed to release the tapes. Then, in the face of protests even from Republicans that the investigation had to be handled by a special prosecutor, he named lawyer Leon Jaworski to replace Cox. The independent investigation of Watergate was under way once more. ◣

The weekend following the Saturday Night Massacre, protesters gathered near the White House urging Congress to impeach Nixon and remove him from office.

Nixon's Fall

Late in October 1973, Nixon's lawyers told Judge Sirica that two of the requested tapes did not exist. Many people assumed that meant Nixon had destroyed them, and more newspapers called for him to resign. Three weeks later came an even more damaging piece of news: The tape of Nixon's meeting with Haldeman, just three days after the Watergate arrests, had an 18½-minute gap.

Despite this, the tapes that were turned over caused enough damage. Late in November, special prosecutor Jaworski and members of his team listened to the tape of the March 21, 1973, meeting of Nixon, Dean, and Haldeman. The tape meshed with Dean's retelling of events—not the president's. They heard the president discuss and approve paying hush money to Hunt. They also heard him tell Haldeman how to answer questions without committing perjury. Jaworski later said that this tape convinced him that Nixon was guilty of crimes. Meanwhile, the House of Representatives took action on an impeachment resolution. On February 6, 1974, the House of Representatives instructed the Judiciary Committee to begin considering impeachment.

On March 1, 1974, the grand jury issued indictments charging John Mitchell, H.R. Haldeman, John Ehrlichman, Charles Colson, and three lesser figures with various charges of conspiracy and obstruction of justice. The grand jury also secretly named the president as an unindicted co-conspirator. That did not formally charge Nixon with any crimes. It did, however, mean that the prosecutors could hand over the evidence they had—including the tapes—to the House Judiciary Committee, which could use it in its investigation into the impeachment question. The House Judiciary Committee wanted more tapes, though. On April 11, committee members voted to request tapes for more than 40 conversations. Jaworski also asked for more tapes—64 of them.

IMPEACHMENT PROCESS

Impeachment is the two-step process for removing a president from office. First, the House of Representatives must vote to impeach the president, charging him or her with high crimes and misdemeanors. Then, a trial takes place in the Senate, with the chief justice of the U.S. Supreme Court presiding. All the senators act as the jury. They must vote whether to convict or acquit the president. If two-thirds vote guilty on at least one charge, the president will be removed from office. Two presidential impeachment trials have been held—Andrew Johnson in 1868 and Bill Clinton in 1999. In both cases, the guilty vote fell short of the two-thirds majority, and the presidents remained in office.

On April 29, 1974, Nixon made a national television address. With a pile of bound transcripts sitting next to him, Nixon said that he was handing over not the actual tapes but typewritten, edited transcripts. In a show of confidence, he declared:

If read with an open and a fair mind and read together with the record of the actions I took, these transcripts will show that what I have stated from the beginning to be the truth has been the truth: that I personally had no knowledge of the break-in before it occurred, that I had no knowledge of the cover-up until I was informed of it by John Dean on March 21, that I never offered [pardons to] the defendants, and that after March 21, my actions were directed toward finding the facts and seeing that justice was done, fairly and according to the law.

In April 1974, Nixon announced he was releasing edited transcripts of the tapes. Within a week, the transcripts were being sold in book form, allowing the public to read the president's conversations.

The president's hope that the edited transcripts would satisfy everyone and end the investigation was misguided. Much of the public, many newspapers, and even several Republican members of Congress expressed dismay over what the tapes revealed. More important, the legal battle continued. The House Judiciary Committee members insisted that they receive the actual tapes. So did Jaworski.

Nixon, meanwhile, began listening to some of the tapes. After hearing one of his earlier conversations, he decided that he would fight to the end to prevent their release. Nixon told Chief of Staff Alexander Haig that he would never let anyone listen to the tapes.

At Jaworski's request, Sirica issued an order demanding that the White House turn over the tapes. Nixon's lawyers appealed to the U.S. Court of Appeals. Jaworski asked the U.S. Supreme Court to hear the case. The court agreed and set July 8, 1974, as the date on which it would hear arguments in *United States v. Richard M. Nixon.*

THE PUBLIC RESPONSE TO THE TRANSCRIPTS

The transcripts showed heavy editing. Some parts of conversations were replaced with the words "material unrelated to presidential action deleted." Others were replaced with the words "expletive deleted." Many Americans were shocked by how frequently these expletives, or curse words, flowed from the mouths of the president and his advisers. Even some Nixon supporters were bothered. The *Chicago Tribune*, a conservative newspaper, issued a call for Nixon's resignation stating, "We saw the public man in his first administration and we were impressed. Now in about 300,000 words we have seen the private man and we are appalled."

On July 24, 1974, the U.S. Supreme Court issued its decision in *United States v. Richard M. Nixon*. Eight justices—including three named to the U.S. Supreme Court by Nixon—unanimously declared that the president must turn over the tapes. The court concluded that Nixon's claim of executive privilege did not extend to these conversations because no vital matters of national security were involved. Further, it said, the tapes were needed to ensure that criminal cases were handled fairly in the courts. Later that day, Nixon announced he would obey the court's decision and turn over the tapes.

That same day, the House Judiciary Committee began televised debates of the articles of impeachment against Richard Nixon. Chair Peter Rodino began by pointing to the oath of office that Nixon, as all presidents, had pronounced on taking office. In it, the president swore to preserve, protect, and defend the U.S. Constitution. This president, the chairman said, had violated that oath. For the next two days, members of the committee read opening statements. Some defended Nixon. Some, including a few Republicans, stated they would vote to impeach.

After a pointed debate, the committee then voted 27-11 to approve the first article, which charged the president with obstruction of justice. Two days later, the committee approved by 28-10 an article charging the president with abuse of power. A third article also passed. It said the president had shown contempt of Congress in not supplying the tapes that had been subpoenaed. A third of the Republicans had joined all the Democrats in voting for these three articles, showing that Nixon had lost the support even of members of his own party. Two more articles, on matters unrelated to Watergate, were voted down.

The House Judiciary Committee was led by Chair Peter Rodino (seated beneath flag) and helped by counsels John Doar (front left) and Albert Jenner (front right).

On August 1, 1974, Nixon decided that he had to resign. Frank talk from leading Republicans made it clear to him that he had no chance of surviving an impeachment trial in the Senate. But he wanted a few days so he could tell his family and closest friends. That weekend, he had tearful meetings with his wife, his two daughters, and their husbands.

On Monday, August 5, the transcript of the taped conversation from June 23, 1972, was released. That was the conversation Nixon had with Haldeman just a few days after the arrest of the burglars. In it, Nixon agreed with the plan to have CIA Director Vernon Walters tell Acting FBI Director L. Patrick Gray to block the investigation. The transcript revealed what many supporters said had been lacking—the smoking gun, or clear proof, that Nixon knew about and had approved the cover-up. The Republicans on the Judiciary Committee who had voted against impeachment changed their minds. The president, they said, was guilty.

On August 8, 1974, Nixon gave his final television address to the nation. He said:

> *I have never been a quitter. To leave office before my term is completed is abhorrent to every instinct in my body. But as president, I must put the interest of America first. America needs a full-time president and a full-time Congress, particularly at this time with problems we face. ... Therefore, I shall resign the presidency effective at noon tomorrow.*

After Nixon told his family of his decision to resign, his daughter Julie Nixon Eisenhower hugged him.

The next day, Nixon bid a tearful farewell to the White House staff. As Nixon and his family left the White House for their California home, Gerald R. Ford was sworn in as the 38th president of the United States. Speaking to the nation, Ford said, "Our long national nightmare is over."

After Watergate

Richard Nixon's resignation did not end the saga of Watergate. Various aides of the president were tried for their roles in approving the break-in or taking part in covering it up. Some, too, were tried for their roles in the break-in of Daniel Ellsberg's psychiatrist's office. Many of those trials ended in guilty verdicts.

The five burglars served several months each in prison. E. Howard Hunt and G. Gordon Liddy, the planners of various break-ins, served the most time in prison—33 months and 52 months. John Dean, Charles Colson, Jeb Magruder, and Herbert Kalmbach all spent from four to eight months in prison, as did some other White House staffers. John Ehrlichman, H.R. Haldeman, and John Mitchell served about 19 months. All those who were lawyers lost their licenses to

practice law. Maurice Stans, who had paid out cash when told to, was only fined. Former Attorney General Richard Kleindienst pleaded guilty to not cooperating with the Senate but never had to serve a sentence.

Vice President Gerald R. Ford (left) was sworn in as the nation's only unelected president by Chief Justice Warren Burger.

Richard Nixon never went to jail. On September 8, 1974, one month after Nixon announced his resignation, President Ford pardoned him of all crimes he may have committed while in office. Ford explained that he did not feel Nixon could receive a fair trial. In addition, he said that a trial of Nixon would once again divide the country and that the nation would lose credibility with foreign governments.

Ford said that his decision was best for the nation. Still, it hurt him politically. Two years later, he lost his bid to win the presidency in an election when he was defeated by Jimmy Carter. The pardon of Richard Nixon still bothered many voters.

Some Watergate figures later enjoyed considerable fame. John Dean became a frequent guest on talk shows, where he offered opinions on legal and political matters. G. Gordon Liddy became a popular political speaker and radio host, known for his strong conservative views. Charles Colson became a born-again Christian while in prison and spent the following years speaking about and working to achieve prison reform.

Nixon wrote several books, mostly presenting his thoughts on important issues facing the country, especially regarding foreign policy. Over time, his reputation improved. When he died in 1994, President Bill Clinton spoke approvingly of him:

> *He gave of himself with intelligence and energy and devotion to duty. And his entire country owes him a debt of gratitude for that service. Oh, yes, he knew great controversy amid defeat as well as victory. He made mistakes; and, they, like his accomplishments, are part of his life and record. But the enduring lesson of Richard Nixon is that he never gave up being part of the action and passion of his times.*

Washington Post reporters Bob Woodward and Carl Bernstein had played an important role by writing many news stories that kept Watergate and the cover-up in the public mind. They wrote two best-selling books about the Watergate story and the last days of the Nixon White House. Bernstein later left *The Washington Post* for other jobs in journalism. Woodward stayed at the paper and became one of Washington's most influential journalists. He also published many best-selling books detailing the inner workings of various presidential administrations.

In 2005, Nick Jones (right) read a statement to the press in which he confirmed that his grandfather, Mark Felt, was Deep Throat. He was the knowledgeable source relied on by reporters Woodward and Bernstein.

Every few years, Woodward and Bernstein—along with some of the participants in Watergate—join historians and journalists to discuss the impact of Watergate on American politics and society. A question frequently asked about Watergate is whether the system worked. Did the courts and Congress protect the U.S. Constitution and people's rights? The consensus among political thinkers and historians is that it did. It was the certainty of a conviction in the Senate, not newspaper headlines, that in the end forced Richard Nixon to leave office. The outcome of Watergate showed the importance of the rule of law, which insists that no one— no matter how high his or her position—is above the law.

Although the system worked, Watergate left scars. The lies and illegalities of Watergate added to the mistrust many Americans felt toward the government as a result of the Vietnam War. Watergate contributed to the attitude that government statements need to be viewed skeptically. Some said that it is a good thing for the press and the public to question what the government says.

WATERGATE AND THE LANGUAGE

After Watergate, political writers attached the suffix *-gate* to virtually every scandal that followed. The scandal also donated some memorable phrases, including John Dean's "cancer on the presidency," Howard Baker's "What did the president know, and when did he know it," and Richard Nixon's "I am not a crook," which he declared in November 1973.

Historian Michael Beschloss pointed out that this skepticism had bad effects as well:

> *The presidency [now] is a weaker office, and it certainly doesn't have the moral authority that it once had before Richard Nixon came there.*

This more skeptical approach to government officials was clearly shown by journalists. Watergate combined with the Vietnam War to change the nature of journalism. Reporters became much more skeptical about the statements and motivations of government officials. Many, inspired by Woodward and Bernstein, investigated instances of misconduct by government officials. Some observers worried, however, that the pursuit of scandals could be destructive by distracting reporters from more important stories.

An immediate result of Watergate was a new law regulating campaign financing. Concerned by the way Nixon aides misused campaign funds, Congress put tighter controls on raising and spending campaign money. But that campaign finance reform law eventually led to new kinds of abuses, which caused the need for other reform laws. This sequence of events suggests that the lasting legacy of Watergate is to remind Americans that they must always be on the watch for abuses of power, because they are likely to occur again. ◣

Timeline

November 6, 1968
Richard M. Nixon is elected president of the United States in narrow victory.

June 13, 1971
The New York Times begins publishing the Pentagon Papers.

July 23, 1971
Nixon approves Huston Plan; approval is later taken back.

September 3, 1971
Plumbers unit enters offices of Daniel Ellsberg's psychiatrist.

January 27, 1972

G. Gordon Liddy presents $1 million intelligence plan and is told to scale it back.

February 21, 1972
Nixon begins his historic trip to China.

March 1, 1972
John Mitchell leaves job as attorney general to head CREEP.

March 30, 1972
According to Jeb Magruder, Mitchell approved Liddy's plan to wiretap the DNC.

April 7, 1972
New rules on fund-raising take effect.

May 22, 1972
Nixon begins first visit by a president to the Soviet Union.

May 28, 1972
Burglars hired by CREEP break into DNC headquarters at Watergate to plant telephone bugs.

June 17, 1972
Burglars return to change one bug and take pictures; they are caught and arrested.

June 19, 1972

The Washington Post carries story linking James McCord to CREEP.

June 22, 1972
Nixon meets with H.R. Haldeman; agrees to cover up plan of telling FBI to stop the investigation because the CIA is involved.

June 28, 1972
John Dean gives acting FBI Director L. Patrick Gray files from E. Howard Hunt's White House safe, saying they include political dynamite.

July 5, 1972
Watergate grand jury begins meeting.

July 10, 1972
Alfred Baldwin, questioned by the FBI, names Hunt and Liddy as being involved in burglary.

September 15, 1972

Grand jury indicts five burglars, Hunt, and Liddy.

November 7, 1972

Nixon is reelected in landslide.

January 8, 1973

Hunt pleads guilty to involvement in break-in and wiretapping.

January 15, 1973

Four of the burglars plead guilty to break-in and wiretapping.

January 20, 1973

Nixon is inaugurated for second term.

January 27, 1973

Peace agreement is signed in Paris, calling for end of U.S. involvement in Vietnam War.

January 30, 1973

McCord and Liddy are found guilty of break-in and wiretapping by jury.

February 7, 1973

Senate votes to set up select committee to investigate Watergate.

February 17, 1973

Gray is nominated as permanent director of the FBI.

February 28, 1973

Gray admits he gave John Dean FBI files about Watergate.

March 19, 1973

McCord writes Judge John Sirica saying that defendants were pressured not to talk and that Watergate was being covered up.

March 21, 1973

Dean tells Nixon of cancer on the presidency; Nixon reinforces decision to give hush money to Hunt.

April 27, 1973

Amid reports that he destroyed files, Gray resigns as acting FBI director.

April 30, 1973

 Nixon announces resignations of Dean, Haldeman, John Ehrlichman, and Richard Kleindienst.

May 17, 1973

Senate Watergate committee begins hearings.

May 28, 1973

Archibald Cox is named special prosecutor.

June 25–28, 1973

 Dean tells Senate Watergate committee that Nixon knew of cover-up.

July 16, 1973

Alexander Butterfield reveals existence of White House tapes.

Timeline

July 17–18, 1973

Senate Watergate committee and Cox ask Nixon to hand over some tapes.

July 23, 1973

Nixon refuses to hand over tapes, claiming executive privilege.

October 10, 1973

Vice President Spiro Agnew resigns after pleading no contest to tax evasion charges.

October 19, 1973

Dean pleads guilty to one charge of obstructing justice in return for promise to help investigators.

October 20, 1973

Saturday Night Massacre: Elliot Richardson and William Ruckelshaus resign; Cox is fired and special prosecutor office ends.

November 1, 1973

Nixon names Leon Jaworski as new special prosecutor.

November 21, 1973

Sirica told of 18½-minute gap in tape of June 20, 1972.

December 6, 1973

Gerald Ford becomes vice president.

February 6, 1974

House votes that Judiciary Committee should look into impeachment.

March 1, 1974

Federal grand jury indicts Mitchell, Haldeman, Ehrlichman, Charles Colson, and three others.

April 30, 1974

 Nixon releases edited transcripts of various tapes.

July 24, 1974

U.S. Supreme Court unanimously rules that Nixon must turn over tapes; House Judiciary Committee begins public debate on impeachment.

July 27, 1974

House Judiciary Committee approves first article of impeachment; two more are later approved.

August 5, 1974

Nixon releases transcript of June 23, 1972, smoking gun conversation that wipes out remaining support for him in Congress.

August 9, 1974

Nixon resigns; Ford is sworn in as president.

September 8, 1974

Ford grants pardon to Nixon.

May 31, 2005

W. Mark Felt is revealed as Deep Throat.

On the Web

For more information on *Watergate*, use FactHound.

1 Go to *www.facthound.com*

2 Type in this book ID: 075652010X

3 Click on the *Fetch It* button. FactHound will find Web sites related to this book.

Historic Sites

The Richard Nixon Library & Birthplace
18001 Yorba Linda Boulevard
Yorba Linda, CA 92886
714/993-5075

The library includes a Watergate gallery.

National Constitution Center
525 Arch St.
Independence Mall
Philadelphia, PA 19106
215/409-6600

This site helps visitors understand the U.S. Constitution.

Look For More Books in This Series

The Collapse of the Soviet Union:
The End of an Empire
ISBN 0-7565-2009-6

Miranda v. Arizona:
The Rights of the Accused
ISBN 0-7565-2008-8

The Little Rock Nine:
Struggle for Integration
ISBN 0-7565-2011-8

The New Deal:
Rebuilding America
ISBN 0-7565-2096-7

McCarthyism:
The Red Scare
ISBN 0-7565-2007-X

Watergate:
Scandal in the White House
ISBN 0-7565-2010-X

A complete list of **Snapshots in History** titles is available on our Web site: *www.compasspointbooks.com*

Glossary

articles of impeachment
formal charges of misconduct by a president or certain other U.S. officials

bail
sum paid by a person who has been arrested and charged with a crime so he or she can be released from jail until the trial is held

convention
national meeting of a political party, where members choose candidates for president and vice president

cynical
having a scornful attitude toward ideals

executive privilege
the idea that the executive branch of the government, including the president, does not need to reply to some requests for information from Congress or the courts

impeachment
the process begun when the House of Representatives formally accuses the president of high crimes and misdemeanors; the president is then tried in the Senate and, if found guilty by two-thirds of the senators, is removed from office

Pentagon
building in Arlington, Virginia, that houses the main offices of the U.S. Department of Defense

perjury
the crime of deliberately lying when testifying in a trial under an oath to tell the truth

pragmatic
based entirely on practical concerns rather than moral principles

search warrant
document issued by a judge that allows police to search property where they expect to find evidence about a crime

segregation
dividing people into different areas because of their race

subpoena
power of Congress or a court to demand that evidence be provided to it

Source Notes

Chapter 1

Page 14, line 19: Bob Woodward and Carl Bernstein. "GOP Security Aide Among Five Arrested in Bugging Affair." *Washington Post* 19 June 1972, p. A01.

Chapter 2

Page 24, line 10: Fred Emery. *Watergate: The Corruption of American Politics and the Fall of Richard Nixon.* New York: Simon & Schuster, 1995, p. 35.

Page 25, line 26: Ibid., p. 48.

Chapter 3

Page 33, line 16: G. Gordon Liddy. *Will: The Autobiography of G. Gordon Liddy.* New York: St. Martin's Press, 1980, pp. 266–267.

Chapter 4

Page 35, line 12: Jeb Stuart Magruder. *An American Life: One Man's Road to Watergate.* New York: Atheneum, 1974, p. 260.

Page 37, line 21: "Transcript of a Recording of a Meeting Between the President and H.R. Haldeman in the Oval Office on June 23, 1972, from 10:04 to 11:39 A.M. " *Nixon Presidential Materials.* 20 March 2006. http://nixon.archives.gov/find/tapes/watergate/wspf/transcripts.html, p. 4.

Page 38, line 7: Kevin Hillstrom, ed. *Watergate.* Detroit: Omnigraphics, 2004, p. 17.

Chapter 5

Page 50, line 6: James McCord. Letter to Judge Sirica. 19 March 1973. *The Watergate Files.* Gerald R. Ford Library & Museum. 20 March 2006. www.fordlibrarymuseum.gov/museum/exhibits/watergate_files/content.php?section=1&page=c&doc=1, p.1.

Page 52, line 5: "Transcript of a Recording of a Meeting Among the President, John Dean, and H.R. Haldeman in the Oval Office, on March 21, 1973, from 10:12 to 11:55 A.M." *Nixon Presidential Materials.* 20 March 2006. http://nixon.archives.gov/find/tapes/excerpts/watergate.html, p. 33.

Source Notes

Chapter 6

Page 63, line 6: *Watergate: The Corruption of American Politics and the Fall of Richard Nixon*, p. 363.

Page 63, line 14: Theodore H. White. *Breach of Faith: The Fall of Richard Nixon*. New York: Atheneum Publishers, 1975, p. 302.

Page 65, line 22: *Watergate: The Corruption of American Politics and the Fall of Richard Nixon.*, p. 370.

Page 70, line 28: *Watergate*: *The Corruption of American Politics and the Fall of Richard Nixon,* p. 50.

Chapter 7

Page 74, line 6: Richard Nixon. "Nixon's Release of Watergate Tapes." *watergate.info.* 29 April 1974. 20 March 2006. www.watergate.info/nixon/74-04-29release-of-tapes.shtml

Page 75, sidebar: *Watergate: The Corruption of American Politics and the Fall of Richard Nixon*, p. 430.

Page 78, line 24: Richard Nixon. "Nixon's Resignation Speech." *watergate.info.* 8 Aug. 1974. 5 April 2005. www.watergate.info/nixon/resignation-speech.shtml

Chapter 8

Page 82, line 20: Bill Clinton. "Remarks by President Clinton at Richard Nixon's Funeral." 27 April 1994. *Richard Nixon Library & Birthplace.* 20 March 2006. www.watergate.info/nixon/94-04-27_funeral-clinton.shtml

Page 85, line 3: "'A Third-Rate Burglary': Twenty-Five Years Later." *OnLine NewsHour.* PBS. 17 June 1997. 20 March 2006. www.pbs.org/newshour/bb/white_house/jan-june97/Watergate_6-17.html

SELECT BIBLIOGRAPHY

Bernstein, Carl, and Bob Woodward. *All the President's Men.* New York: Simon and Schuster, 1974.

Emery, Fred. *Watergate: The Corruption of American Politics and the Fall of Richard Nixon.* New York: Simon and Schuster, 1995.

Gerald R. Ford Library & Museum. *The Watergate Files.* www.ford.utexas.edu/ museum/exhibits/watergate_files/index.html

Hillstrom, Kevin, ed. *Watergate.* Detroit: Omnigraphics, 2004.

National Archives and Records Administration. *Nixon Presidential Materials.* http://nixon.archives.gov/find/tapes/watergate/wspf/transcripts.html

White, Theodore H. *Breach of Faith: The Fall of Richard Nixon.* New York: Atheneum Publishers, 1975.

Woodward, Bob. *The Secret Man: The Story of Watergate's Deep Throat.* New York: Simon & Schuster, 2005.

FURTHER READING

Barron, Rachel. *Richard Nixon: American Politician.* Greensboro, N.C.: Morgan Reynolds, 1999.

Holland, Gini. *The 1960s.* San Diego: Lucent Books, 1999.

Schlesinger, Arthur Maier, Fred L. Israel, and David J. Frent, eds. *The Election of 1968 and the Administration of Richard Nixon.* Philadelphia: Mason Crest Publishers, 2003.

Sobel, Syl. *The U.S. Constitution and You.* Hauppauge, N.Y.: Barron's Educational Series, 2001.

Sobel, Syl, and Pam Tanzey. *How the U.S. Government Works.* Hauppauge, N.Y.: Barron's, 1999.

Stewart, Gail. *The 1970s.* San Diego: Lucent Books, 1999.

Index